LET'S CELEBRATE KWANZAA!

Written and Illustrated by
Arielle Phoenix

Copyright © 2019 by Cyber Phoenix LTD
All rights reserved.
This book or any portion thereof may not be reproduced or used in any manner whatsoever without the express written permission of the publisher except for the use of brief quotations in a book review.

First Printing, 2019
Paperback ISBN 9781704585659

Cyber Phoenix Books,
London, United Kingdom

email arielle@cyberphoenixltd.com
www.books.cyberphoenixltd.com
www.cyberphoenixltd.com

TABLE OF CONTENTS

What is Kwanzaa?..............................4

The Seven Principles of Kwanzaa..........7

Kwanzaa Symbolism...........................25

Get into the Spirit of Kwanzaa..............27

Kwanzaa Family Fun..........................31

WHAT IS KWANZAA?

Kwanzaa is a Pan-Afrikan holiday which celebrates family, community and culture; created in 1966 by **Dr. Maulana Karenga**

Dr. Karenga is an African-American professor, author and activist who was also a prominent figure in the **Black Power Movement** of the 1960s.

When he created Kwanzaa, his goal was to establish a holiday, for the African-American diaspora; to **celebrate and embrace their heritage and culture, give thanks and prepare for a fruitful year ahead.**

He believed through celebrating our roots we would be **proud** of our Afrikan heritage and appreciate the many struggles of our antecedents.

Although it was originally created for the African-American community, Kwanzaa is now embraced and celebrated by black people all around the world and serves as a reminder that we are all connected and we will always have a reason to celebrate and give thanks.

"Kwanzaa" derives from the Swahili phrase **'Matunda ya kwanza'** which means **'First fruits of the harvest'** or more simply 'first fruits'

Kwanzaa is seven days long and is celebrated from December 26th to January 1st.

On each of the seven days of Kwanzaa the family will light a candle, discuss and participate in activities that relate to the principle and theme for that day.

Many people assume that Kwanzaa is a replacement for Christmas and that celebrating one means you cannot celebrate the other. While this is true for some, this is not the case for everybody.

The celebration of Kwanzaa tends to unite Afrikans based on our commonalities and, as such, irrespective of your religion, political standpoint, tribe or any social community you belong to you can embrace and include Kwanzaa in your annual traditions.

"Kwanzaa is not a religious holiday, but a cultural one with an inherent spiritual quality,"

Dr. Maulana Karenga

NGUZO SABA

The Seven Principles of Kwanzaa

The 7 Principles of Kwanzaa

1. Umoja - Unity
2. Kujichagulia - Self-determination
3. Ujima - Collective work and responsibility
4. Ujamaa - Cooperative economics
5. Nia - Purpose
6. Kuumba - Creativity
7. Imani - Faith

December 26th - Day 1
UMOJA
UNITY

To strive for and to maintain unity in the family, community, nation, and race.

Family is a gift.
There is the family that you are born into,
and the family that you choose.
There are family members and ancestors that you will never meet;
and family that you will lose.
When we celebrate the principle 'Umoja'
we are choosing to acknowledge and value each other.
We are choosing to embrace and celebrate ourselves,
wherever we may be in the world.

Today you could all write some poetry on the theme 'unity' and share or go to see a live show or theatre performance together.

December 27th - Day 2
KUJICHAGULIA
SELF DETERMINATION

To define ourselves, name ourselves, create for ourselves, and speak for ourselves.

On this day, Kujichagulia, it is the perfect moment to read and learn about great Afrikan achievements. You can study black history in your town or country or you could explore great Afrikan achievements across the seas.

Whatever interesting stories and facts you discover, you can share with the rest of the family during dinner.

Self-determination is a key principle because if you know who you are, other people's projections, expectations and objectives cannot affect you.

Kujichagulia is all about character-building and growth. This is why learning about the advancements of some of our ancestors is a great place to start. It reveals the journey and obstacles we might need to face in order to achieve our goals.

December 28th - Day 3
UJIMA
COLLECTIVE WORK AND RESPONSIBILITY

To build and maintain our community together and to make our Brother's and sister's problems our problems and to solve them together.

'The Story of Ubuntu'

The story of ubuntu really puts ujima into perspective and the two are closely related. This story displays what it looks like when you value oneness and teamwork and actively practice it.

One day, an anthropologist who was studying an Afrikan tribe decided to play a game with the children of the village.

He gathered some sweets and put them all in a big basket and then called all of the children over.

He explained the game to them.

"The first one who makes it to the sweet basket gets to keep them all!"

The children looked at each other and smiled as they took each others hands and ran in unison towards the sweet basket.

They all arrived at the same time and divided the sweets equally amongst each other.

The anthropologist was shocked and asked the children why they had decided to run together instead of racing each other and winning all of the sweets.

The children replied,

"Ubuntu. How could any one of us be happy when all of the others are sad?"

December 29th – Day 4

UJAMAA

COOPERATIVE ECONOMICS

"To build our own businesses, control the economics of our own community and share in all its work and wealth."

Do you have an idea for a business or project you could start with your friends or family?

"Let's not do it just to survive, but let's do it as a strategy to prosper..."
- W.E.B Du Bois

"PARDNER"

A group of people decide that each week they will put away a specific amount of money. This collection is called 'a hand'. After a set period of time one person collects all of the money and they repeat this until everybody gets their sum of money (draws pardner). They decide who will act as the banker and be in charge of this arrangement. So, for example, if 10 people are in the group and throw a hand of £100 weekly, over the next 10 weeks the banker will pay £1000 (the draw) to one person each week until everybody in the group has drawn pardner.

December 29th - Day 4
UJAMAA
COOPERATIVE ECONOMICS

Capitalism has always been one of the biggest contributors to inequality and as such, cooperative economics has been used throughout history as a means of growing and maintaining finances, building businesses, buying a house or simply surviving.

During slavery, for example, even though reading was illegal - black slaves who could read would teach others. They understood how important it was that this skill was passed on and the opportunities having it may present. Similarly, on Sunday's, which was a day off, of sorts, they would collectively farm small gardens and share the produce amongst themselves. In some cases, they would save to buy each other's freedom!

This is also where Jamaicans got the concept for the 'pardner (partner) system' - saving collectively. Afrikan slaves would use pardner money to buy their freedom. In even more recent history, in the United Kingdom, during the Windrush period, those in the Afro-Caribbean community used pardner to help them finance all kinds of things. This old, Afrikan tool for liberation is still used today.

Modern-day cooperative economics is still very much about survival but even more so, it is about prosperity.

December 30th - Day 5
NIA
PURPOSE

We all have a purpose, during our journey of life.
It could be one or two or as many as five.
So many options and ladders to climb,
but ask as many questions you need, to help you decide.

Nia is a day for deep thought and reflection.

Each year during Kwanzaa, ask yourself these questions and write your answers down in your diary. You do not need to know all of the answers now, just have a think:

What makes you happy?
If you could do anything at this moment, what would you do?
Who makes you laugh the most?
Where do you want to live?
What do you look forward to when you wake up?
Where do you want to travel to?
If you were to open a shop, what would you sell?
Who would you like to meet?
What makes you feel loved?

December 31st - Day 6
KUUMBA
CREATIVITY

To do always as much as we can, in the way we can, in order to leave our community more beautiful and beneficial than we inherited it.

Creativity is celebrated all throughout Kwanzaa and the entire family can get creative together through story-telling, poetry, music, cooking, drawing and so much more!

Here are some ideas for creative activities you can do:

1. African necklace making with beads or painted pasta.
2. African inspired papier-mâché masks
3. Unity flag making using various bits of red, black and green cloth or made using coloured card.
4. Song making (you can use instruments, computers or just household objects!) The songs are guaranteed to be family hits you can perform each year.
5. Baking and decorating Kwanzaa themed cookies
6. Writing your own African inspired poetry and stories.
7. Weave your own red, black and green mkeka with coloured paper or card.
8. Create your own board game. Come up with a concept pamoja (together).

January 1st - Day 7
IMANI
FAITH

To believe with all our heart in our people, our parents, our teachers, our leaders, and the righteousness and victory of our struggle.

Imani is "a profound and enduring belief in and commitment to all that is of value to us as a family, community, people and culture."
- Dr. Maulana Karenga

If we embody this level of faith we will value ourselves, each other and our communities and never seek to imitate what is outside of us.

We will become innovators, inventors and influencers.

It is always important to remember that each and every one of our ancestors who fought vehemently through the struggle did so with faith in a better future.

A good exercise to try today might be the 'Trust Fall'
Fold your arms, close your eyes and fall backwards into the other persons arms.

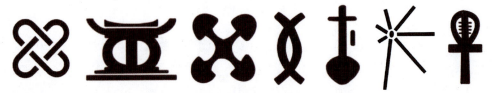

Everybody can practice these principles and use them in their day-to-day operations.

If applied, the seven principles establish a solid foundation for the advancement and growth of the individual and collective black people all over the world.

Kwanzaa Symbols and Their Meanings

KWANZAA SYMBOLS

1. MKEKA = KWANZAA MAT
The mkeka is used as the foundation and it represents our culture, tradition and history and therefore, the basis on which we build.

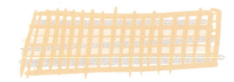

2. MAZAO = THE CROPS
Crops are a key part of traditional Afrikan harvest celebrations as these are symbolic of the rewards of productive and collective labour.

3. KINARA = KWANZAA CANDLE HOLDER
This is symbolic of our roots and our ancestors.

4. MUHINDI = CORN
This is symbolic of our children and our collective future.
Even if a family celebrating Kwanzaa does not have children, the corn is still used as acknowledgement of our children as traditionally, it was understood that it takes a village to raise a child.

KWANZAA SYMBOLS

5. MISHUMAA SABA - SEVEN CANDLES

These seven candles represent the Seven Principles of Kwanza. Each candle is a symbol of a principle. Three of the seven candles are red, representing the bloodshed and the struggle. Another three are green, representing hope for the future and the last candle is the black one which is placed in the center of the kinara and represents the united Afrikan people.

6. KIKOMBE CHA UMOJA - CUP OF UNITY

This is symbolic of the 'foundational principle and practice of unity which makes all else possible.

7. ZAWADI - GIFTS

These are symbolic of the labour and love of parents and the commitments made and kept by the children. Gifts can be used to acknowledge the accomplishments of the child and also encourage them for the new year ahead.

GET IN THE SPIRIT OF KWANZAA!
DJEMBE

The djembe drum is around 800 years old and originates from 12th century Mali.
The name 'djembe' derives from the phrase "Anke djé, anke bé" which means "everybody gather together in peace" in Bambara; the native language of Mali.

A handmade Djembe drum is said to hold three spirits within it. That of the tree from which the wood came to craft it, that of the animal who's skin was used to cover the head of it (typically a goat) and that of the craftsman who made it.

The Djembe drum is sometimes called the devil drum. For no reason other than the fact that it was traditionally made with the wood from a tree called Dimba (also known as devil wood)

The djembe has been used throughout history to communicate long distances between tribes.

IF YOU ARE LUCKY ENOUGH TO OWN A DJEMBE, BE SURE TO PLAY IT DURING KWANZAA!

GET IN THE SPIRIT OF KWANZAA!
BENDERA YA TAIFA
Flag of the Nation

The red, black and green Pan-Afrikan flag of liberation has many names but they all represent the same concept: Unity.

The flag was first introduced by Marcus Garvey, founder of the UNIA (United Negro Improvement Association), in the 1920s.

In one of his 'Negro World' newspapers, around that time, he wrote 'Show me the race or the nation without a flag, and I will show you a race of people without any pride.'

KWANZAA FAMILY FUN

Scan and copy each activity.

The first one to complete wins! Or, you could complete them together like the children in The Story of Ubuntu.

Across
1. The activist, author and professor who started it.
2. Try to stay on beat!
3. Given on January 1st.
4. Symbolic of the rewards of productive and collective labour.
5. A savings system our ancestors used to buy their freedom.
6. Collective work and responsibility.
7. Encouraged all throughout Kwanzaa.

Down
1. An ear for each child in the family
2. Represents our roots and ancestors
3. Kiswahili word for faith
4. Define yourself so nobody else can
5. A framework for black excellence
6. "How can any one of us be happy when all the others are sad"
7. The first principle.

How Many Words Can You Make From:
CELEBRATE KWANZAA

What you need:
Paper, pen.

Rules:

 Set the timer for 1 or 2 minutes.

 You must only use a letter once.

🔺 1 point per letter in the word. 🔺

🔺 Whoever has the most points wins! 🔺

Go!

LET'S CELEBRATE KWANZAA!

```
U J A M A A V N W K H F U C N P R F
P I Q D J E M B E K I N A R A M V F
A N C E S T O R S A K A R E N G A A
W R F K U J I C H A G U L I A S N M
W D Z K H I B G A R V E Y P P B D I
Y T E O B L U J I M A S N A K R B L
C E L E B R A T E I M A N I D Y H Y
L T U M O J A P R O S P E R I T Y U
A Z A W A D I V D K U U M B A J E C
U B U N T U J E K F L A G U W S R C
O R S L K W A N Z A A V N I A R G Y
M L B L E U N I T Y C U P V I U P W
```

Find the following words in the puzzle.
Words are hidden → ↓ and ↘ .

ANCESTORS
CELEBRATE
DJEMBE
FAMILY
FLAG
GARVEY
IMANI

KARENGA
KINARA
KUJICHAGULIA
KUUMBA
KWANZAA
NIA
PROSPERITY

UBUNTU
UJAMAA
UJIMA
UMOJA
UNITYCUP
ZAWADI

About The Author

Arielle Phoenix is a mother of two, dedicated to creating a plethora of unique, fun and educational cultural children's books. She began creating flash cards and writing books to help her children learn Swahili and soon noticed there was a need for multicultural and bilingual children's books. Today, she produces books in seven language pairs and plans to add even more to the list.

www.books.cyberphoenixltd.com

Download more free Kwanzaa games @ www.blackhomeschoolforum.com!

Made in the USA
Monee, IL
19 December 2022

22903966R00021